Things I Learned From My Patience...

CW00820324

Olivia Guerini

BookLeaf
Publishing

Things I Learned From My Patience... ©
2022 Olivia Guerini

All rights reserved.

No part of this publication may be reproduced, stored in a retrieval system, or transmitted, in any form or by any means, electronic, mechanical, photocopying, recording or otherwise, without the prior written permission of the presenters.

Olivia Guerini asserts the moral right to be identified as author of this work.

Presentation by *BookLeaf Publishing*

Web: www.bookleafpub.com

E-mail: info@bookleafpub.com

ISBN: 9789357618984

First edition 2022

To all those who have shared their pain with me
- thank you.

ACKNOWLEDGEMENT

This book wouldn't be possible without all the team at Reality Wellness Group in South Africa; A 24/7 Trauma informed call centre that I managed from 2018 - 2020.

In addition, Rethink Mental Illness as well as CareTrade Charitable Trust have formed part of my UK home and created a platform for me to connect with others.

Lastly, all my personal support structure - you helped me maintain my sunshine and helped me keep stock on myself in an unjust world.

PREFACE

I have written poems of my reflections on what I have learned from clients that have used various services I worked with.

These poems include words and phrases that have been said by actual people who access mental health services for grief, trauma, addictions, navigating relationships and work related stress. I have not distinguished between South African and UK Clients to showcase that humans all connect on a level that transcends oceans and borders.

I hope you find comfort, recognition and the same awe into human resilience, that I experienced.

Thoughts and Prayers

You send your thoughts and prayers
You send them all one by one
But thoughts and prayers do nothing
When they're up against a gun

You say its so awful and terrible
BUT be grateful they are all alive
We will send more thoughts and prayers
That will help your family survive

You hope the trauma ends quickly
You say God's will kept them all safe
Where was God when they were tied up
With metal bindings causing skin to chafe

You send your wishes and prayers
You tell me I must be strong
I wasn't there right? It can't be that bad
I needn't worry now... nothing is wrong

I ask for help, you lend a smile

And send thoughts and prayers my way

Will thoughts heal the welts on my
grandmothers arm

Will prayers keep the fears at bay

Keep your thoughts please. They are no use now
Keep your prayers away from us too
And if misfortune ever comes your way
I'll send my thoughts and prayers to you

Rest on my bones

I was born into this life
Empty, broken and not having a clue
Having no clear direction
Of what I was even put here to do

I've been burned. I've been tortured
twisted in every direction that hurt
Until my brain bent and buckled
I believed I was destined to be treated like dirt

You had similar scars and pain
I recognised the look of survival in your eyes
Loving also seemed to come easy to you
The force of it often took me by surprise

I fought against the gentle stubbornness
Afraid of falling - fearing the drop from the sky
But I owe it to myself to lean into trust
To rest on my bones; albeit they're both brittle
and dry

All the things they've said

Don't fight so much... It doesn't hurt
Don't try to turn your head
I archive my fear. Bookmark my horror. I ignore
my body's scream of protest
And pay attention to all the things they've said

What's wrong with you? You are so uptight
You're so dirty. Clean up where you have bled
Don't cry - you wanted this after all!
I acquiescence to all the things they've said

You will like it more if you just relax
Come lie with me in my bed
I can make you feel different. Special
I tried to smile at the things they've said

My body no longer fights off the pain
I can keep myself safe and separate inside my
head
But my nightmares are always leaking
Bursting from all the things they've said

What's my name

I call distressed. My phone pressed to my ear
I hear "HELLO? How can I help you, my dear?
Already, I am annoyed and I breathe inwards,
feeling my frustration rise
They start the script of telling me that
confidentiality always applies

I try to start my story. This will take effort. This
will take all my might
I'm interrupted "What's your postcode? Have
you called us before tonight?"
I start listing off details. My GP, Address - none
pf the constructs of who I am
Interruption bursts through the phone "Are you
going to kill yourself? DO you have a plan?

Are these people reading a script? Do they even
know I am there
And if I had a plan to die tonight, would this
person even care?
10 minutes have already passed now, the woman
says firmly to me
Have I tried bathing with my clothes on? Can I
just make a cup of tea?

I feel the tears forming. I want comfort. I don't need more tasks
But with every command and action given, I feel my body brace. My voice mask
The call is finishing now. I am told I can always call again
But I know they don't care. They are not there to connect. She didn't even ask me, my name.

The tale of my grief

The clouds don't hold the same shape anymore
The stars don't hold their appeal
Time rolls out in like an endless path
The blood in my veins have turned to steel

Time froze the moment you left
Music lost its melody
There aren't enough words in the english
language
To explain what you mean to me

I've cursed the ground and now face dread
Of getting through the day
I never knew pain had the power
To take layers of your skin away

Together we could drink in moonlight and steal
the sun
But now I can't even bear the rain
I dont crave normalcy, balance and calm
Because I had fallen in love with a hurricane

We have danced through lightning and braved
the storms
But I could see that you were losing your spark

I wish you could see the impact you made on us
That unforgettable, searing mark

You braved the world with such grace and poise
You carried others pain in your hand
But you carried an unbearable pain of your own
A pain that we could never understand

And when you chose to set us both free
My heart and spirit broke in two
Life now seems unimaginable
Nothing holds my interest without you

So I'll search the earth for life once more
I'll cross oceans to stay sane
I'll live the life that you left for me
And follow the path that leads me to you again

You can't save them

I weep for the broken, the desolate, the afraid
They are born into tragedy. No one coming to
their aid
The homeless, the destitute, the terrified, the
scorned
So many people broken, bleeding. Wishing they
were never born

People ask for help. They are met with tick
boxes and forms
How do you fill in the dotted lines when your
insides feel ripped and torn
Remembering diagnoses, refilling your
medication scripts
Applying all those coping skills. Laying them
down brick by brick

There are addicts with their vices. There are
insomniacs with their pain
They take medication to make themselves numb
now. Dial down the volume of their brain
It is hard to see such suffering, witnessing it day
by day
It can be hard to make space for pain. To fit all
that healing in a day

And I weep because we cannot all be saved. You
can only love them where they stand
You can't transform them, only console them
Only extend one of your available hands.

I can take on all your pain

Do you need distraction
Do you need a vice from the pain that you feel
Because I can be your court jester
I can give your mind a break from that hamster
wheel

Try not to stare at my bones and my flesh
They're etched with the words from my tribe
Instead lean into the solace I give
I will give you a place to run and hide

My skin can cover yours. Its thin and it drapes
It doesn't bleed and make such a mess anymore
I may choke on my fumes as I give our more
love
I'll never make you feel like a chore

I don't want you to suffer. I can swallow all that
hurt
I'll pull myself apart to entertain your soul
You will never know if I've hit empty or if I'm
afraid
I always try to stay in control

Bring me your pain. Ill stuff if nice and deep

I'll give you relief from the ache in your veins
Bring your demons. Unload them them into me
I'll take on all your pain

Curiosity and Fun

Don't stare at the moon and stars too long
Their gaseous exchanges will leave you reeling
You're only human, its not your fault after all
That you like to turn a memory into a feeling

You want hope. You try to run from despair
But you lose sight of yourself along they way
Its only when heaven presses against your lips
And stands there, begging you to stay

Who can blame you for being restless
With the cosmos bleeding in your veins and
bones
You sense apathy and feign interest
You fall asleep to your life's dulcet tones

You need to dance on the grass again. Fall asleep
in the meadows
You need to reconnect with the clouds and sun
Don't forget to lose sight of who you are
You can ignite yourself with curiosity and fun

Picking

I pick and pick at my skin
I pick and pick until it bleeds
Pulling, grabbing, scratching, ripping
It satiates the pain that my anxiety needs

I hide my nails in the sleeve of my jacket
I am embarrassed of the outline of my nails
I can laugh and tell everyone I am fine
But my blood fingers drip emotional betrayal

I pull at my hair, grabbing strand by strand
I don't even realise what I am doing till it hurts
And you see me absentmindedly unravelling
myself
Trying to undo anxiety's curse

I try to stop. I promise I do
But it seems like every week, I drop the ball
And I pick and I pick, and I pull and I rip
Until one day, there will be nothing left of me at
all

Welcome to Adulthood

Welcome to adulthood. We hope you enjoy your stay
Did you pack your coping skills? Have you come a long way?
We see you requested a bedroom, one that has a view
We see you requested a small room. One that doesn't have space for two

You're going to have to leave some childish comforts behind
We will need to tip out your thoughts and take an inventory of your mind
Let's see. I can see a fear of strangers. Mmmm, we best let that stay
But I can see hope and wonder. Let me take that - keep it out of your way

You can your take low self-esteem with you. You can buy more in 3 years time
I can see your motivation looks off colour. Better pickle it in anxiety-brine
Abandonment issues can be hung up in your closest. Alongside your need to be alone

15

We can always add some distracting apps, and
save them to your phone

Weird body hair will arrive tonight. Mood
swings will come too
You can expect a slower metabolism with weird
things happening when you go to the loo
I think that will be all for now. Ignore existential
fear that sometimes gets in they way
Welcome to adulthood. We hope you enjoy your
stay

The things I did not break

Remember to breathe deeply. Drink all your
water. Eat your fruit
Take vitamins, buy a night light. Learn to play
an instrument. No, not the flute
Sit in therapy. Do the work. Reorganise the
voice in your head
Drink a cup of tea. Breathe through the dread

Everyday I wake up, I recover from my dreams
I am tortured. My family murdered. My soul is
ripped apart at the seams
I start the day with coffee. Cut out the sugar. Eat
gluten free bread
Check my phone for notifications. Ignore
calendar updates making me feel scared

Push onto the train. Push off. Push down the
stairs
Complete my to-do list. Ignore the homeless.
Avert my eyes from their glare
Take my tablets. Go to the gym. Ignore the way
my body aches
And try and supress the way I wish I was not
responsible for all the things that I did not break

The pandemic

The world needed a break you see

A break from you and a break from me

From cars and trains and noise and smoke

From the things making wildlife choke

The people needed to slow down their day

So the earth had some time to say

That it was hurting from machines and their works

That human mess leaked into the sky and into the dirt

And humans needed also needed rest and space

Because they were making a mess all over the place

So one by one they each slowed their roll

And a new virus formed and took its toll

And it made them scared and their hearts ache

But our fragile earth needed a break

So don't worry about later. Don't worry about
then

Once our earth has healed, we'll be ok again

Preparing for love

My neurons knew trauma
Before I even knew how to smile

And my body understood being let down
And being abandoned once in a while

I'm prepared for torture, bankruptcy and crime
I've planned every death that I'll ever see

I know how to look at nightmares in the eye
And I know how to look after me

I'm used to being forgotten, being laughed at
and being hit
I prepare for shame and embarrassment too

But there's nothing in the realms of each or the
heavens
That could have ever prepared me for you

Curious

Don't stare at the moon and stars too long
Their gaseous exchanges will leave you reeling
You're only human, its not your fault after all
That you like to turn a memory into a feeling

You want hope. You try to run from despair
But you lose sight of yourself along they way
Its only when heaven presses against your lips
And stands there, begging you to stay

Who can blame you for being restless
With the cosmos bleeding in your veins and
bones
You sense apathy and feign interest
You fall asleep to your life's dulcet tones

You need to dance on the grass again. Fall
asleep in the meadows
You need to reconnect with the clouds and sun
Don't forget to lose sight of who you are
You can ignite yourself with curious and fun

What the people say

We are born to rely on others
Born to have our mothers make us feel alive
We have to communicate our needs
If we are ever going to truly survive

Our first task is trusting
Trusting that others will come when we call
We have to regulate our emotions
When we are met with silence... Just no response
at all

We then need to learn independence
Attach joy in the art of hearing our name
Be praised for the tasks we can do alone
Or feel ridicule, fear and shame

We then need to take initiative
Either rising to praise, or receiving
condemnation to make us wilt
We either feel incredible pride at the things we
can do
Or we cut ourselves open on our father's second
hand guilt

We learn responsibility, social norms

Adapting our behaviour day by day
Is it any wonder we often fall apart
On the basis of what other people say?

How does it feel?

How does it feel?
When you can't trust your own brain
When you have to take medication
Just so you can feel sane

How does it feel?
When, as soon as you open your eyes
You have panicked thoughts and quickened
breath
Terror thinly veiled in a disguise

How does it feel?
To always bury constant worry
To bump into things, to cry at silly things
To punctuate every interaction with the word
"Sorry"

How does it feel
When your catastrophic thinking grows
When people who are let are thought to be dead
When pretending to be OK is the headlining
show

When you ask me how it feels
It is hard to use words that fit

Because having anxiety is feeling like you are
dying
But you just have to get on with it

The Little Things

I have learned to love the little things
That I see about myself
The way my eyes light up
When I see my favourite chocolate on the shelf

The scar on my left knee
That I got when I was two
The way I tie my laces
Using the method I was taught to use

I am starting to love the little things
Like the ringlets of my hair
The tattoos on my hips, the piercings in my ears
Scars that I chose to put there

And all these things I love about myself
Will help pave my road ahead
Because the past roads leading me here
Wanted me to hate myself instead

Unstable Ones

There is a fear in society
Even a society as modern as we are
That the people who have battles with their mind
Are to be feared

Those people who have intrusive thoughts
And who scale mental health like a triage
Are the ones society looks at and leers

The unstable are the ones who sit in emotional
mess
But take the time to confront it every day
And the unstable are the ones who always do
their best
But you do your best to stay out of their way

With minds more intricate than you could ever
dream
And more resilience than you would ever
understand
Who's demons would beat you down, causing
you to burst at the seam
Pulling all your resources, incessantly, on
demand

Its the unstable ones you see - who are the
soldiers of our time
Fighting the same struggles as you and
simultaneously fighting their mind
Reality testing before you've even finished your
tea
Hoping their vices will let them go, let them free

Climb into their mind one day
I dare you - take a peak
Because being an unstable one
Is not for the weak

You're not welcome here

A man sat alongside a busy street
Collected his change, tucking his coat over his
ears
People walked around him with an upturned
nose
Their averted eyes said "you're not welcome
here"

With outstretched hands and a pleading look
Some people avoiding her, some looking over
with a sneer
The store manager comes out shaking his fist
Telling her "you're not welcome here"

An elderly couple are playing the flute
Hoping someone will pay them for their musical
cheer
But their bodies seemed to just get in everyone's
way
Their stomach grumbling "you're not welcome
here"

A mother begging with a baby strapped to her
back
She ran away from her husband in fear

But her bruises and filth turned them all away
And onlookers muttered "you're not welcome here"

Night-time falls, it's time to sleep
An elderly man sits down while young boys throw stones and jeer
You're ruining out streets with your cardboard box
Go away, you're not welcome here

A woman combs the bins for food
Passers-by mutter with a polite veneer
Why can't she just get a real job?
Her type just isn't welcome here

Tired and weary, no shelter from the rain
A small family huddle under an old wooden pier
A policeman stops and ushers them all along
Telling them quite plainly "you're not welcome here"

Having no possessions, no home, no job
Doesn't make you any less of a person – let's be clear
I hope you remember your humanity
Before you mutter "you're not welcome here"

God's Will

Dear pastor I am writing to you
Because there's a few things I'm trying to
understand
How do you reconcile a world in torment
Saying that this is all God's Plan

See, I've read the bible and I've heard your
sermons
But there are so many things that don't quite
make sense
I can see you're getting angry - so just hear me
out
I am not hear to cause any offence

See, the first thing I don't understand
Is how God is full of power and full of love
But the world is in complete disarray
And there's just radio silence from the "big man"
above

Now I know that you say God has a will and a
plan
But I don't understand how his mercy plays out
Because he is either too weak to save children
from despair

Or our pain is something he just doesn't want to
know about

I am sure you can appreciate
That believing in a God is a difficult thing to do
When people die of hunger everyday
And cancer riddles the bones of innocent
children too

And even if we take the horrors of the world
And put them aside for a minute, to reflect
The bible actively encourages slavery
Oh, sorry that's in Exodus - or did you forget

Perhaps, let us take the Bible, Minister
And turn to Genesis 19 versus 31
Here you see incest is acceptable
As Lot used his two daughters to try and give
him a son

You seem uncomfortable Bishop, Should I stop?
Or can I draw your attention to Mattew 21
versus 18 - 23
Here your kind and patience Lord and Saviour
Had a temper tantrum with a harmless tree

I guess you don't like examining the bible
I guess I take it all out of context too

Should we focus instead on the lies of the
Church
Or do you have something better to do?

Let's start with the Catholic Church
And how it covered up thousands of cases of
abuse
And many priests were protected from justice
Some were detained and later, let loose

I noticed you have no tax return forms
I also notice your offering baskets brimmed with
notes
Oh, you're using that to upgrade the church's
carpark?
Not to helping failing charities struggling to
keep afloat?

I can see you're done with this conversation now
Seems that you're done talking to me today
I would tell you to go to hell Preacher,
But by the looks of it, you already know your
way...

About Me

In my mind - it is tangled
A voice says "I hate you. I hope you die"
I push it down. I still wake up
I ignore the feeling of wanting to cry

I have felt panic for as long as I can remember
A feeling of anxiety. A feeling of dread
I remember never feeling good enough
Having to work extra hard to try and get ahead

When asked to write a poem about me
My brain laughed and tipped out junk onto the
keys
I guess hating me is an easier task
Than giving me space to face my lived atrocities

I have had Heartache
I have had sorrow
I have had triumph
And joy too

But when your first memories are of loss and
shame
It is a hard narrative to undo

I am woman
I am flesh
I am exquisite
I am a mess

I am in the middle of a story
At the end of my rope
I am always doing better
I am doing my best to cope

Ten years from now
I hope I find it easier. To be kind when I think
about me
I hope I feel pride. I hope I feel happy
I hope to find myself somewhere where the sky
meets the sea

Milton Keynes UK
Ingram Content Group UK Ltd.
UKHW020433131223
434231UK00015B/868